Brave
Resilient
Beautiful

Cover Design by Samantha Vence
Photography by Etienne Surrette
Edited by Claudia Cramer of CSC Professional Editing & Creative Writing Services
* Some of the names used in this book have been changed.

Printed in the United States of America

Dedication

This book is dedicated to my daughter, Victoria. I am very proud to be your mother. From the day you were born, you have inspired and challenged me to be a better person. You are a true gift to our family. No matter how old you are, you will always be our "Princess Buddy." I pray you never lose your adventurous and compassionate spirit.

I also want to dedicate this book to every teenage girl I have had the privilege of mentoring and growing with over the years. You will always hold a special place in my heart.

Acknowledgments

I want to give a shout out to some amazing people and influences God has placed in my life:

First of all, thank You Jesus for Your goodness, grace, mercy and love for me. You make my life worth living; You drive me with purpose and passion.

Thank you to my college sweetheart, the father of my children and amazing husband, Scott. Thank you for being the most fun person I know, and for leading our family with such integrity. Your drive to follow God's heart is an example to our family and I am thankful for the overcomer that you are. Love you Boo!

Thank you to my wonderful parents, Dave and Sandy McLucas. Thank you for teaching me to how to pray and trust God always. Thank you for being yourselves and for setting an example of what it means to love others.

Thank you to my siblings: Katie, Mark and Kara. No matter how much life changes, we always have each other, and for that I am so thankful. Thank you for being all-around rockstars and for all the love. More importantly, thank you for letting me boss you all around! Love you!

Thank you to Terry Walker, Barb Gundry Erickson, Jannette Coco, Liz Allman, Nato & Lemy Mercado, and all of the adopted big brothers and sisters who always speak life into me.

A huge shout out and thank you to Samantha Vence and Becky James for helping a sister out with all of my technical and computer- illiterate issues.

Thank you to Claudia Cramer of CSC Professional Editing & Creative Writing Services for editing this project.

Thank you to every friend, and every one of my many cousins, who listened to my crazy ideas, or who listened to me talk non-stop at sleepovers (until everyone else would fall asleep.) I would be the only one left talking.

Lastly, thank you to every mentor who directed or redirected me. I would not be who I am today without those who have loved me genuinely. I guess that's why love is the greatest commandment. When we truly love one another, it is a very powerful thing.

Thank you *all* from the bottom of my heart. I am so very grateful for all of you.

Contents

Foreword   From My Heart   9

One   Change Is Good   17

Two   Finding God In Everyday Life   85

Three   Forgiving Others   118

Four   Loving Yourself   137

Five   What's Your Story?   145

Foreword
From My Heart

Hello Gorgeous! Thank you for choosing to read this book. I am so excited to share my heart with you!

One night while I was laying in bed (big and super- pregnant with our third child), the Holy Spirit spoke to my heart and told me to write this book for *you*. I was like, "Lord, whaaatt??? Uhhhhh??? Me??? Are you sure???" I waddled myself out of bed and paced around my house praying. I argued with God for a minute...or two...or okay....an hour. "I'm not qualified to write a book, God!" But when God speaks I know I better listen! So I obeyed, and started writing this book the very next day. Throughout this book, I have written about some of the experiences I had as a teen, and what those moments taught me.

Seriously though, the main reason that I wrote this book is obedience to Him, not putting my life on a pedestal. This book is written for *YOU*! Hopefully it will inspire you, encourage you, motivate you, and get you thinking a little (or a lot) differently.

I strongly believe that what you can make of your life, and getting the most out of it, is all about having the right perspective. Having God's perspective!

God wants you to enjoy your life to the fullest. I believe God's desire is that you would always move forward in life, no matter what circumstances come. Your life is your story. A story that tells of a *Brave*, *Resilient* and *Beautiful* girl! A girl who faces life's challenges head on, with Jesus by her side. A girl who rises above all of life's situations and circumstances. One who understands her true beauty and worth through God's eyes.

Your life's journey...your story is being written right now, as you live the life God has designed *just* for you.

I learned some life lessons at a very young age. Lessons that maybe made me have to grow up a little quicker, but that was the journey on which God had me. That's why I want to share my story with you.

Girls, I believe you are in one of the greatest learning stages of your life. You have an opportunity to grow and learn. You have the opportunity to overcome circumstances and issues that you may face now or already have faced in your teen years. I believe you can change your thought process, grow, learn and mature right now!

Don't get caught up just living moment to moment, or day to day thinking you will deal with things and change when you "grow up." The process can start now.

Jeremiah 1:5- *I knew you before I formed you in your mother's womb. Before you were born I set you apart and appointed you as my Prophet to the nations.*

Before you were born, your Heavenly Father knew you. Think about that for a minute. You were thought of by God! What you look like, your hair color, your talents, your personality, your passions, your dreams... and the list goes on... Every detail about you was designed by God! How exciting it is when you truly start to embrace that fact? This is why no two people are exactly alike.

Can you imagine how boring it would be if everyone in the world looked alike, dressed alike, enjoyed the same foods, played the same sports and had the same talents and abilities? Our differences good or bad, make the world what it is today. A very fascinating place!

This is why it is important for you to embrace who *you* are. It is important for you to learn from the journey you are on and embrace who God created you to be.

Before you start reading the rest of this book I want you to stop and think for a second.

Think of at least five things you like about yourself. Don't be shy, come on! You've got some great qualities!

1.

2.

3.

4.

5.

List three things you'd like to change:

1.

2.

3.

What are three goals you have for your life?

1.

2.

3.

This is just to get your thoughts moving and focused on developing yourself while reading these pages.

Now, write a prayer note to the Lord asking Him for help with what you need. Tell Him how you are feeling.

Lord,

Love,

_____

(your name)

Here is my prayer for you:

I pray that as you grow in God you would understand that He sees into the depth of your heart and nothing is hidden from Him. So, I pray that you don't hold back from Him. God already knows you inside and out so just talk to Him. He is not looking for perfection. He's looking for a heart that is open and desires to grow and serve Him. I pray your eyes would be opened. I pray that an excitement for who you are created to be, would rise up within you! My prayer is that you embrace being a *Brave, Resilient and Beautiful* girl. I believe the best is yet to come for you, girlfriend!

Love,

Kelly

Alright Girly... Let's Do This!

Chapter 1
Change Is Good

Most people I have met over the years struggle with change. *Change* means to make something different or to cause a transformation. *Change* for you could mean changing schools, starting a new job, getting your driver's license, being allowed to date, experiencing a divorce in your family, losing a loved one or moving to a different home or town. Even changing your hairstyle or rearranging your room is a form of change!

Change can be big or small, but the beautiful thing about change is that it equals growth. Anytime you are outside of your comfort zone, adjusting to something different or experiencing a feeling you have never felt before, you have the opportunity to grow! I *say opportunity* because you have to be willing to fight the uncomfortable feelings change can bring. Often times, you will have to fight the enemy (the devil) from beating you down and playing a sad song over and over again in your head. I believe God wants us to experience change in our lives regardless of how uncomfortable it may be!

Check out this verse:

Isaiah 64:8- And yet, O Lord, You are our Father. We are the clay, and You are the potter. We all are formed by Your hand.

This verse reminds me that God is the potter and we are the clay. As He forms us into who He wants us to become, we *are* going to experience change. We might think we have life and ourselves all figured out, but then God can say... "Nope! I need to tweak this a little more..." Or, "I would like to bring this particular quality out more." Think about it. How boring would it be if every day, every interaction and everything we experienced was the same? Every day would be like the movie, *Groundhog Day*! Have you ever seen that movie? It's an old movie that I used to love to watch. Basically, the main character in the movie goes to sleep and wakes up in the same day over and over again until it drives him nuts! Funny for a movie, but for reality? No. thank you!

I am glad each day holds something new. I am glad that each one of us is different. I am glad that we get to go on this adventure called life. That's the way we have to embrace it. Head on. Fierce and BRAVE. Slay girl, slay!

Now, I don't say these things to you from a place of *rarely* experiencing change, living somewhere off in *La-la Land*. My life has been nothing *but* change since the day I was born.

I like to call all of the changes in my life, adventures. The truth is if I had not stayed close to Jesus through it all, I could have easily become a resentful, angry and depressed girl. Maybe you can relate. Maybe you have also been through a lot of changes at a young age. I really hope you connect to some of the stories I share, and gain a new perspective on the life God has given you to live!

My adventures began in Ocala, Florida where I was born. Ocala is also the place where my parents met and where they eventually were married. Sunny, pretty Florida, where a lot of people want to move or vacation. I have vague memories of living there, but I do remember walking through a short path in the woods near my house to get to my Aunt Deb's house. Aunt Deb was always up early and I was always able to play with my cousins Stephanie and Stephen at her house. My little sister Katie was just a baby then; she was not a very good sleeper, so my mom would try to sleep in when she could. This gave me great opportunities to take it upon myself to slip out to go play over Aunt Deb's.

I was always a bit independent, and I'm sure I thought I could make my own decisions at three years old. I was just doing my thing. You know, just walking with my baby doll, through the woods to Aunt Deb's house. No biggie, right? Ha! Needless to say my Mom was not too happy with me for taking off like that! Sunny pretty Florida. That was home... for a minute.

I was born into a family with "roots" in ministry. Meaning, a whole lot of my family members are/were pastors or missionaries. When I was a little girl, my parents felt God asking them to go into ministry as well. They decided to follow God's plan for their lives, and accepted a position at Bethel Assembly of God in Newark, New Jersey. Bethel was the church that my Grandfather was the pastor of at the time, and my parents really had a heart to reach the city for Jesus.

Mom and Dad packed up our home, our family of four and we all said our goodbyes to Florida. My parents trusted God to provide every step of the way and were anticipating what was to come in our new place. Even at a young age, I was always very aware of things that were going on around me. The details of life I can remember are amazing. (Well, I guess *amazing* is one way to put it, but it's actually a little crazy how much I can remember!)

We were all happy once we got settled into our new home. I remember seeing graffiti for the first time and being totally fascinated by it. I thought it was beautiful! There were a lot more sidewalks than I'd ever seen before, and I remember asking the question: "What is that?" a lot. When I tell people that I used to live in Newark, sometimes I get reactions like, "Eww, why would you want to live there?" I'm not going to lie: when I get those reactions, I get a little annoyed on the inside.

I guess I feel annoyed because living in Newark was a major time of growth and happiness in my life, despite some of the city's reputation. At the time, Newark was full of violence, theft and drugs. There were definitely no palm trees or sandy beaches there... True, it was not the safest place, but it was home.

I loved the diversity of people; I loved always being around and going to sleep at night to the sounds of the city. From day one of starting ministry there, my parents worked as a team. They always made my sister Katie and I feel like we were on the team too. Katie and I went everywhere with our parents, and we were often given small jobs we could do to help. It was living in Newark that started my personal journey as an elementary school-aged girl.

When we first moved there, we lived in my grandparents' house. It was a little chaotic and crazy, but we managed. My dad was finishing up Bible College, as well as working at the church. During the week, Dad traveled to Pennsylvania for college, and then drove back home to New Jersey on the weekends. My uncle Chuck had started a private school within the church, and Katie and I attended school there. It was nice having all of our family around every day. My grandmother even ran the lunchroom at the school, so that meant a whole lot of Swedish Fish and Reese's Peanut Butter Cups from the snack bar for me! Thank you Lord for Reese's Peanut Butter Cups (just sayin')!

After a short time, we ended up moving out of my grandparents' home, and actually started living in an upstairs apartment of a nursing home. Yes, that's right... a nursing home! A retired couple owned a huge house that was used to house the elderly. It looked like an old mansion! The owners were family friends, and they were kind enough to let us live in the upstairs apartment for a while.

I can still remember the smells of that place...and let me tell you, the smells were so random. I would walk in from school through the smoking room, then into the kitchen where food was always cooking and past the sitting room where I'd get a good whiff of something else too... if you know what I mean. There was a grand old stair-case we walked up and down to get to the apartment. Katie and I used to beg to ride the motorized seat that went up and down the stairs, but it just never happened.

We ate our dinners in the dining room with all of the residents. Oh, how those old ladies loved pinching my cheeks. They also loved telling Katie not to pick her boogers. Imag-ine having a bunch of grandmothers under one roof.

You know, some people may have been em-barrassed living in a nursing home. Maybe some would have been embarrassed to eat their meals in the dining hall with the other residents. I was young when I experienced this living situation. I know firsthand that when you are young, sometimes it's easy to take on the attitude of those around you. If my mother would have been embarrassed to be there, then chances are I would have been embarrassed also. If she would have complained about it, then maybe I would have too. Instead, I remember my mother looking at our circumstances as a blessing. She never complained or felt sorry for our situation. We were *shown* to be thankful. We were thankful to the family who was kind enough to allow us a place to stay, and thankful for the delicious food we got to eat every night.

You know, it is so true... if you count the blessings in your life, and determine not to focus on the bad things, you will start to view life a little differently. That sad and depressed feeling you might feel just starts to fade away. Even when negativity is around you, you can still choose to count your blessings. When you make a decision to quit complaining about your situation and comparing it with others, God can really start to work in you and make you who He wants you to be!

When our time living at the nursing home ended, Mom, Dad, Katie and I all moved to Valley Forge Christian College. We only lived there on the weekdays while my Dad was at school. This way, we wouldn't have to be separated for so long.

We all moved into an apartment on campus, and once again we were setting up house. My mom has said now that the apartment we lived in was very tiny. It's funny, because one of my most favorite rooms I ever shared with Katie was in that apartment. Dad had made Katie and I bunk beds out of old church pews and cut out a heart shape as the headboard. They were pink and white. Mom hand-painted the words "Jesus Loves Kelly" on my bunk, and "Jesus Loves Katie" on Katie's bunk. I've always loved the color pink, not to mention hearts, so those beds were pretty cool to me!

Katie and I were both so excited that those beds were carefully made *just* for us. God really blessed our family through other people that year. I remember Mom being so excited because someone had left groceries at our door one day. After all, my Dad was eating condiment sandwiches for lunch. If you don't know what a condiment sandwich is... it's a sandwich made of bread, ketchup, mustard and mayo. Ramen noodles were never called ramen noodles at our house. They were always called "Good Noodles." Because seriously, who doesn't love those guilty pleasures of salty goodness? They are gooood.

We all traveled back to Newark every weekend for the youth service and two Sunday services. Katie and I would fall asleep on the old blue church bus as my parents drove a lot of the teens home on Friday nights after youth group.

Even though I did not have a lot of material things, my life experiences were rich and pretty cool. I was getting to live in two places at once. I was around my parents' youth group with teens who I looked up to and who treated me like I was their little sister. Since Newark was just across the river from New York City, my dad would take us there often, just to walk around. We would eat an NY hot dog, ride the Staten Island Ferry and look at the Statue of Liberty. Anything cheap or free is what we usually did in the city, and those experiences are worth a million bucks in my opinion.

Eventually my dad finished his time at the college, and we were able to move into a more permanent home. It was a multi-family home that the church had bought so that their pastors could have a place to live. My family moved into the upstairs level which was its own little apartment. My grandparents moved into the main level and my aunt, uncle and four cousins moved into the basement apartment. Those years were fun living together in that big house! We would have sleepovers and sneak into Grandpa's ice cream. You could see the New York City Skyline in the distance from my grandparents' living room window, and we would "skate" in our socks over the marble floor in the entryway.

See, my life has been changing ever since I can remember. But with every change, something good eventually would come out of it. When you can learn to embrace change and learn from every moment in your life, you will learn things that cannot be found in a book.

I'm writing a book about the lessons I learned at a young age, but remember my experiences won't be the same as yours. Your everyday life is what you learn from most. The problem is that you are tempted to shut your bedroom door, turn on sad music, read unrealistic things on social media, loathe in negativity, and somehow think by doing these things you will eventually feel better about life. It won't work! It's a trap from the devil, and girls... I want you to see beyond that nasty trap!

One day, my parents announced to us that we were going to be moving away from Newark. I don't think I really knew what to feel. I was young and didn't know too much about life outside of the city. It sounded exciting, but I was scared at the same time. Dad told us all about a church in Georgia that really needed a pastor and he felt like our family was supposed to go there.

Let me tell you, when we announced to our church that we were moving, I had never before seen so many people cry in all my life! The church gave us a going away party and people just cried and cried and cried. I remember trying to quietly cry like an adult and just dab my eyes with tissues... but that didn't work. I ended up ugly crying like a kid should! Leaving was tough on all of us. Still, we had to pack up our things and move. We moved away from the place I called home. It was the place where I first sang a solo, first acted in a play, first lifted my hands to praise God and first experienced an all-night prayer meeting.

It was the place where I first cleaned a church bathroom, and used Windex on a big glass door. It was where I saw some super-natural things happen through the Holy Spirit, and where I experienced the love of friends who loved like family. It was where I learned how to be street smart and how to jump rope double dutch. It was where I first rode public transportation. It was where si-rens, horns and once in a while, a gunshot were familiar sounds. It was where I real-ized that there are really bad people in the world, but Jesus still loves them. It was also where I learned that there are some really amazing people in the world too.

It was the place where I first ate Spanish rice & beans and pastelillos. It was where I first fell in love with the city. It was also where my little brother, Mark had been born and I experienced babysitting for the first time. So much life and love to leave behind and I had to do just that: Say goodbye.

Within a few weeks, our family moved to the town of Quitman, Georgia. We knew it would be warmer in Georgia, and that Quitman was a small town. Yet, I don't think it really hit home until we got there. Katie and I were city girls. Living in this farm town should not have been appealing to us, but somehow it was! We were like kids who had been caged up and now we were free to run in a field! It was a new adventure!

A family in our new church owned a pig farm. On that farm sat a 100 year old farm house. No one had lived in that old house for many years. The farmer was also a bee-keeper, and he was using the old farm house to keep his bees. So, guess what house we moved into? Yep, you guessed it...the 100 year old bee house in the middle of a pig farm! Home, sweet home! Talk about a culture shock. We went straight from a multi-family house in the city, to a dirt road on a farm, living in an old farmhouse with pigs on all four sides of the house.

Not to mention the chickens. I had never smelled a pig or a farm in my life and it burnt the hairs right out of my nose! What in the world? Where the heck were we? Yet, it was so exciting and adventurous.

There were dirt roads to freely walk up and down without our parents hovering over us like they had to do in Newark. There were hay barns to jump in, abandoned houses to play in and an old cemetery to explore and get all creeped out in. How about seeing little piglets being born? Yep, we got to do that too. There was always a mama pig giving birth, and we would wait and wait to see those little piglets being born. Talk about a change of lifestyle!

Please remember this, girls. There are moments in life when you may wonder how did I get here or why am I here? You could be like me, and you may have to move to a new place that is not necessarily where you want to be.

Or it could be a decision you've made, or a consequence that's causing some unwanted change in your life. When you fully put your trust in the Lord, He will totally use those unwanted moments to make you stronger. He will always have your back! He's got the best plans for you! Until you believe Him for yourself, you will never truly be able to move forward in a positive way.

The changes that had to be made and the adjusting that came with that move to Quitman were so much harder once school started. My sister, Katie and I rode a big yellow school bus for the very first time in our lives. Those were such exciting and nerve-wrecking moments for us at the same time! We were sort of thrown into a place where we knew absolutely no one, except each other. That was a little scary and intimidating. As soon as we set foot on that yellow school bus, we learned what prejudice and racism were for the first time in our lives. We were called "white butts." I didn't really know what that meant, but we were not intimidated at all.

Katie and I were used to street talk from living in Newark. So I replied: "How do you know what color our butts are? Have you been looking?"(which made no sense.) Then Katie pipes up and says, "Shut up, you stupid butts." (Katie was always better with the comebacks.) Then the kids that called us white butts started laughing and one of them gave me a high five. He said, "You alright, girl."

We rode the rest of the way to school, and I stared through the foggy bus window not knowing what to expect next. When I stepped off the bus, I noticed some girls staring me down with a disgusted look. I thought it was because of the oversized sweatshirt of my Mom's that I was wearing, but looking back I now know what it was. It was prejudice and racial tension. It was other white people judging me because I was riding the school bus; there were also people of color on the school bus acting defensively because maybe they assumed we were prejudiced too. That was something I had never experienced in my life. I was always surrounded by other races and cultures in Newark; I loved being around all kinds of people. I couldn't care less what color anyone was. I never thought anyone was any different from me, and the idea that they were *because* of skin color? Geez, that was really hard for me to understand, and I had no desire to be a part of whatever that was. I was taught to love everyone.

Starting a new school in the middle of the school year was an intimidating moment in my life. I had people staring and even making fun of me for having a northern accent. Not fun. All I knew to do was to be myself. It was my first experience being the *new girl.* Several of the girls at school kindly named me Kelly *McDorkus.* Isn't that precious? Oh, kids can be cruel! The Kelly *McDorkus* thing, ended up being ok though, because I made some new friends.

At recess, I was asked to hang out with a group of African American girls. They loved playing with my "golden hair." They kept saying, "Girl, you is so pretty. Give me some of this golden hair!" I loved listening to my new friends talk and sing. One girl named Ramona used to smack her lips and fling her hands around before she said every word. They made me feel *at home* and I loved them! Who cares if I was white 'cause well... I didn't really know what it was to be "white" anyway.

It's amazing because looking back, I could have easily become a withdrawn, unhappy adolescent. I could have let the sadness and pit-of-my-stomach nausea from feeling bullied and out of place consume me. I could have hung my head every time the mean girls would make fun of me, call me names or reject me. But what on earth good would that do? I didn't want to be a sad or mad person.

Did I want to be rejected and hurt? No. However, my desire to enjoy life was greater than my desire to be accepted by a certain group of people. I decided to continue being a smiley, outgoing girl, not afraid of taking in whatever the day would bring. I decided to be *BRAVE*.

It's interesting that the main people who were so kind to me at that school were not white... Yet, some thought I was only supposed to socialize with white people to be accepted. Totally didn't get that one.

Does this topic of racism make you a little uncomfortable? Sorry...But honestly not sorry, because its real, and it still happens today.

We need to talk about things that are uncomfortable sometimes in order to change. God has commanded us to love everyone... and that means EVERYONE! Not just those with whom we are comfortable.

One weekend, I invited one of my new friends (who was not the same color as me) to spend the night for a girls' sleepover. I remember the topic of conversation it was at school that Monday. I almost liked that I was being talked about negatively because of my little sleepover...there is something satisfying about taking a stand for the right thing.

Clearly racism is a learned behavior. My parents loved everyone and never compared or contrasted people in a negative way. Therefore, I didn't either. Prejudice was something I was being exposed to, but it wasn't something I understood at all. It was strange to me. Being in an environment like that was also strange to me at first. It was a very tough adjustment.

Thankfully, our home was filled with faith, love and lots of laughter. Having that environment helped to give me a sense of security. We had frequent family devotions that most of the time I reluctantly sat through.

Our family devotion time was where I learned how to pray. My parents would make us take turns praying out loud. When it was Mom's turn, she would pray for every single member of our extended family...by name... which is a huge amount of people! It felt like it took an hour for her to pray! Man, can my mom pray. I'm thankful that our family kept communication open and we were always reminded that God loved us.

Our new church in Quitman was very loving to and supportive of our family. Our church was also a safe haven for me those first few months of living in a new place. I had never met such friendly people in my life. I was learning what Southern hospitality was, that's for sure. It took a little time, but I was eventually able to make good friendships. Every girl wants those BFF kinds of friend-ships, you know what I mean?

One day, a family dressed stylishly with a daughter around my age, came to our church. I can remember sitting in that orange church pew thinking, I wish I could be that girl's friend! Since our church was so small, it was always obvious when a visitor came. I met Julie Ives that Sunday, and I think we were inseparable after that. The Ives family blessed my life so much. I spent many days and nights in their home and they always treated me like family.

Julie and I loved walking to Pizza Hut and playing the jukebox. We would seriously raid her house looking for change to play that thing. I didn't know if Julie wanted to play it as much as I did, but she always went along with my bright ideas. At home, I wasn't allowed to listen to any music that was not Christian. I would play a lot of songs on that jukebox... preferring anything by Michael Jackson.

Julie and I also spent a lot of our time volunteering at a nursing home. We thought volunteering there was the most fun thing to do! We loved visiting with the elderly. We enjoyed playing games with them, singing to them and hearing their stories. Once in a while, we'd try to visit someone who didn't want visitors. I can remember us running for our lives a time or two!

Julie also didn't mind that I had a major crush on her older brother, Jason. Girls, I honestly thought that if Jason saw me dancing to the Marky Mark and the Funky Bunch song, "Good Vibrations" then somehow he would magically fall in love with me. Sometimes when I would spend the night at Julie's house, I would wait by a big window for Jason's curfew. Does it sound like I was a creeper? Well, I guess I innocently was. I would wait for his Mustang to pull into the driveway, put on some Marky Mark and do my dance, girls! UMMM yes I did. Julie would just sit there staring at me like I was insane! Those silly crushes can make us do silly things sometimes. Those were some good times, and great memories now.

Julie went to a different school than I did, which is probably why we didn't get tired of seeing each other. She was a patient friend, for sure...because I was always coming up with some crazy ideas! Julie was my first close friend in Quitman, but thankfully I made many more friends as time went on.

Living in Quitman was also where I found my voice. My singing voice, that is. I had a love for singing since I was a little girl, but was always too intimidated to let it out. It was at the end of 7th grade where my gift was "discovered."

One day, I stayed after school to help my music teacher, Ms. Wall with some class-room work. Ms. Wall was working in her of-fice, and I asked her if I could sing on the microphone for a minute. She said, "Sure," not ever even looking up from her desk. I went to the mic, and started singing the solo from one of the songs we were learning in choir. Ms. Wall literally came flying out of her office like... "Whattt???" She was shocked that this quiet new girl could sing with so much soul.

Ms. Wall started freaking out and clapping her hands! I was not expecting that reaction from a woman whom I admired so much. What happened next, I really did not expect. Ms. Wall paraded me around the school to sing for the teachers and custodians who were still in the building. Talk about coming out of your shell! I don't think I had a choice!

Ms. Wall gave me the main solo in our next performance and that was my first experience singing on a big stage. I was hooked. As a teacher and mentor, Ms. Wall was such an encourager and she really pushed me out of my comfort zone. Just her belief in me caused me to develop a passion for music.

I was finally loving my new life, my home, my church and school. I even started teaching myself a great southern accent! Words like: *ain't...yonder...hey y'all...*and *fixin* no longer sounded like a foreign language to me. Life was good for the most part. It was home.

God's Word says that He makes all things beautiful in its time.

Ecclesiastes 3:11- Yet God has made everything beautiful for its own time. He has planted eternity in the human heart, but even so, people cannot see the whole scope of God's work from beginning to end.

When we give things time to be different or give ourselves time to adjust to change, things will eventually get better. Even with all of the changes I had gone through, life had finally gotten so much better! I had made a lot of new friends, became very involved in extracurricular activities, had finally adjusted and even started to consider myself a "southern girl."

Then one day, my parents sat us down for a family meeting. They told us there was a possibility that we would be moving...again. Seriously? I was so annoyed. Why were we moving? Why was this "God's will?" Why were we going back to New Jersey? Annnddd... why did the curious adventurous side of me kind of think maybe it could be fun to move again? So many mixed emotions and questions were going through my mind.

A little while after my parents told us that we may be moving, we all traveled to Washington Township, New Jersey to check out what could possibly be our new home.

It's funny; I can remember so much about my life but I do not remember that particular drive to New Jersey. Maybe I was asleep the whole time. Or maybe I was listening to Whitney Houston's *Bodyguard* Soundtrack, and making myself depressed. Probably the second *maybe* because the Whitney Houston songs get me every time! I was probably in the backseat being a depressed teen, feeling sorry for myself for 16 hours.

When we got to Washington Township, I thought it looked like a pretty cool place. I was *trying* my best to look on the bright side. I liked the idea of living back up north, and being close to family and old friends again. I liked the idea of living in a new house and decorating a new bedroom.I liked the fact that I would be living close to New York City again.

Girls, there is always a bright side! You have to force your mind to go to it sometimes. Now, did I *really* want to leave my new friends? Nope. Did I *really* want to start a new school and do all that adjusting all over again? Nope. I had to face reality though. This was happening whether I wanted it to or not!

The following Sunday when the church in Washington Township was taking a vote to see if everyone was in favor of my dad being their pastor... I sat in the car. I did NOT want to accept this change.

However, I had parents that told me to suck it up, and to stop feeling sorry for myself! I rolled my eyes and reluctantly got out of the van to be with the rest of my family. We were all standing outside, and a deacon came out to tell us that the church had voted *YES* in favor of my Dad coming to be the new pastor. Well, I knew what that meant. Moving again!

As our family walked into the church, everyone started clapping as we walked down the aisle. I felt *on display*, and I didn't like it. As I walked with my family down what felt like a mile-long church aisle, I didn't smile or look up at anyone. I sort of wanted to let everyone know that I wasn't happy. My Dad got up on the stage, spoke for a few minutes, and then told the church that he would accept the position as their new pastor. And just that quick...within 24 hrs. Change. Here we go again!

After the service was over, we piled back into our car and started the drive back to Quitman. Two weeks after my parents accepted their new position, we said all of our goodbyes to everyone we had grown to love in Georgia, packed up our house and moved back to New Jersey. We moved away from the place where I first experienced living in the country, first milked a cow, first gathered fresh eggs and first saw a dirt. It was where I first heard a southern accent, where I first experienced prejudice and where I first had to stand up for myself and what I believed in. It was where I first experienced being out of my comfort zone many, many times.

It was also the place where my baby sister Kara was born and where our family was completed. I had grown to love Quitman, Georgia, and I was not a happy camper to have to leave.

The change of moving didn't scare me as much as it annoyed me. I had *just* started high school and it was the middle of the school year. I had *just* gotten the hang of changing classes and figuring out my locker combination for goodness sake! Now, I had to learn all of that again in a new school?! I had no choice really, but to roll with it... And a lot of times in life you have to do just that... roll with it!

When we arrived in New Jersey, we moved into a temporary rental home that was in a very nice part of town. Being back up north was not much of a culture shock for me. It actually made me feel more at home to be back in New Jersey. I *was* feeling pretty depressed for the first month though... The only thing that made the change a little easier for me was that we lived near family and my cousin Renee' again. Even though we were cousins, Renee' was my best friend. We also got to re-connect with a lot of our friends from Newark again. The first few months were a fun little reunion time with all of our friends and family.

When I started school in our new town, it was very intimidating. I was in the middle of my 9th grade year, and high school was still new for me in general. When I finally saw my new school, it felt huge!

The idea of having to find my way through that big school scared me a lot! I had gone from a private school in Newark, to a small school in a small town in Georgia and now to a large school in a progressive area in New Jersey. As I walked into Westwood High for the first time, I felt very insecure in a way I had never felt before.

A soon as I walked into that school, I saw some of the most beautiful dark-haired Jersey girls I had ever seen! Suddenly, I felt *really* ugly. The fact that my teeth were crooked, and that I needed braces, became very real to me in that moment. Suddenly, my clothes felt really out of style too. My big hair, bright makeup and clothes from Wal-Mart were not going to cut it anymore. Yikes! It was not a fun feeling.

I remember tripping up the stairs to get to one of my classes on the very first day of school. My books and papers flew everywhere! So embarrassing! I wanted to cry, but I didn't. People just kind of looked at me as I gathered all of my loose papers and books that had fallen. No one offered to help, or asked if I was ok. There was one kid who was kind and friendly to me that first day. His name was Cory. Cory thought my southern accent was cute...However, I was now faking the southern accent because it wasn't natural for me to talk like that anymore. .I decided to fake the southern accent because people made a big deal about how cool it sounded, and they wanted to hear me say different words. Ha! It was like I was from another country or something.

I ended up sitting by myself at lunch that day. No one asked me to join them. I also didn't eat anything because the simple act of walking through the lunch line alone intimidated me at this particular school. These moments, these insecure, and horribly un-comfortable moments. When change makes you feel like you *can't*... When change makes you feel like you're not good enough, overlooked, lonely, and rejected... These moments are very uncomfortable! These are life changing, character-building moments. Moments where you have a choice to make. Will I let this one day, or this one point in time define me? Will I let it control me? Will I let it get me down? No. Girl, you CAN'T! Remember, it is just a moment. It's not for-ever.

If we let these moments control how we feel and ultimately how we act, they becomes time-wasters. They will get you nowhere every time! You have to push through and keep going. I went home after that first day of school, and also discovered that my sister Katie had felt very similar to me on her first day. I don't really remember much talk about it over dinner or anything... I think I was just trying to understand what I was feeling. I went up to my room after dinner and looked at all of my yearbooks from Quitman. I thought somehow looking at pictures of me and my friends would bring me comfort. I made collages of all of my friends' pictures and hung them on my walls. I guess it made me feel like I had friends.

There was no social media back then. The only way to talk to my friends on the phone was through a long distance call. Long distance phone calls cost money. I had to ask permission and be given a time limit if I was to talk to any of my friends on the phone long distance. I did a lot of letter writing though (where you actually put a handwritten letter in the mailbox.) That was the only consistent option I had at communicating and keeping in touch. So, I wrote, and wrote, and wrote to all of my friends. It was fun going to the mailbox each day waiting for the letters that they would write back to me.

Our new church seemed welcoming to our family. The youth group had a love for God unlike any I had ever seen before! They really loved worshipping and praying together. I was also glad that for the first time I had a youth pastor who wasn't a family member. I was happy to make some new friends in the youth group, but unfortunately none of the girls from the youth group went to my school.

Oh, that dreaded school. The first few months for me were not fun! I was not quiet about the fact that I was a Christian at school, and at first I felt like I was the only one there! Let me just add that it felt like *everyone* in the South was a "Christian." So, it was a reality check when I realized that kids my age were doing things and acting in a whole lot of ways that I was not comfortable doing or acting. The girls' bathroom was where everyone would go to smoke, and it smelled so bad in there! It was always a cloud of smoke when I walked in.

There were girls literally sitting in the bathroom by the dozens, smoking between classes. I had never seen anything like it! It was crazy! Since I didn't want to smell like an ashtray, I would usually just wait to go to the bathroom until I got home.

Once again, I was out of my comfort zone. There I was... in a big school, with supermodels walking around wearing name-brand clothes, smoking in the bathrooms and partying on the weekends. I didn't know how I would *ever* fit in. You know what happened though? I never *did* "fit" in. I always stood up for my beliefs and a lot of times I was made fun of for it. I still smiled at people even though my teeth were crooked, and I decided once again... to just be myself.

Girls, you are uniquely and beautifully you. You are an individual. You are not supposed to be copies of one another! When you can stop comparing yourself and letting others make you feel like you are not good enough...you will win!

God takes us on these journeys where we are faced with having to embrace who we are. You must embrace your looks, body type, your talents, abilities and your personality. Guess what? When you are ok with you, then others will be ok with you too. If they are not, then, oh well. Shake it off!

You see, when we face change, it forces us to dig a little deeper. When we are faced with unknown emotions or experiences, we have no other choice but to literally build a deeper connection with God. Otherwise, life will take us under and drown us.

The devil wants to use our situations and circumstances to kill us emotionally and spiritually. The devil also wants to keep you held back... and you don't want that, do you? I know I sure didn't and still don't!

After a few months of trying to figure it all out, I decided to let God figure it out for me. I surrendered my heart to Him fully and began spending time reading His Word. I listened to music that encouraged me, and started journaling my thoughts and feelings. I fell in love with Jesus and He became my very best friend.

See, a relationship with Jesus can be more than something you just hear about or that you are being told to do. It is real! Jesus IS *your* best friend. But, you can't be best friends with someone you never spend time with, right? You've got to spend time with God! Some ways to spend time with Him are praying, writing your thoughts and feelings to Him in a journal, reading your Bible or devotional or listening to inspirational music. You've got to put that phone down, girly!

Instagram and Snapchat are not going to make you feel better or grow into a better person. Only Jesus can do that, and He will if you give Him some of your time.

As I spent more time with Jesus, He started to help me with my confidence. When 10th grade came, I got my first job and I was able to treat myself to a Gap clearance rack every now and again. I also finally got some white Converse sneakers that every "cool" kid had. The only thing is... someone should have told me that Converse sizes run big because when I bought them my feet looked like clowns' feet.

I honestly didn't really look as "cool" as I had hoped to in my new Converse. As time went on, I had made more friends, started singing at different events and places again and I finally got braces on my teeth! Life was feeling pretty good again! I was feeling OK.

Until one day (cue horror music), my parents sat us down to tell us that we may be moving... again... *back* to Georgia. I was thinking...Okay, whatever parents. Hmmm...more change coming right up! But wait... I didn't order another dose of change. It's like when you were a little kid and your parents made you eat your vegetables. You just had to do it...because they said so. Remember just roll with it? Well, I just had to roll with it...again.

The truth is, my parents were under a lot of stress. Dad was making a lot of changes in the church that the majority of the people did not want. The stress was wearing on my Dad physically and emotionally. My Dad felt like he had done all he could do in leading that particular church. Dad truly felt that God was releasing our family to move on. My parents often talked openly with us about these things. It was important to communicate, so that we could understand as much as we could.

Our family had only been back in New Jersey for about two years. Although I loved living near my cousins and spending time with them... I had not lived back in New Jersey long enough to become super-attached to anyone. More than anything I just kind of wondered *What If?*

I wondered what it would be like to stay and graduate from Westwood High School. I wondered what it would have been like if I would have made the cheerleading squad that I was planning on trying out for the following school year. I wondered how the friendships I had finally made would have turned out to be, and I *really* wondered what it would be like to *not* have to move...ever again.

It's funny how time changes things, right? Remember me saying that before? See, sometimes when we face change it can feel so miserable and we wonder if we will ever make it through... you will. Just hang in there! You're not alone no matter how alone you may feel. Give God time to work in your life. Your feelings are always subject to change. Always remember that.

Whatever you are going through or feeling... just give it some time. Pain doesn't and shouldn't last forever. Somehow, I had actually grown to love my friends *and* my school! What a complete reversal compared to the way I felt when I first moved there. I thought I would never make friends at that school. Some of my friends from school even threw a surprise going- away party for me! That was my first and only surprise party, and I will never forget it. They made me feel so special and loved. It was a priceless moment for sure, and it made it that much harder to think of starting over somewhere new. Still, I had to say goodbye to all of my friends...again.

I said my goodbyes and moved on from the place that I first felt ugly, insecure and inadequate. However, through those horrible feelings, I also learned to feel beautiful, confident and able to do anything with God.

It was the place where I learned that if I wanted to change something, then it was up to me to do so. I learned to stop complaining about the things with which I wasn't willing to take a risk. I was leaving the place where I first took voice lessons, practiced driving a car, worked a job, learned to find Jesus for myself and worshipped with my hands up freely. I was leaving the place where I learned that people can sometimes turn on you if they don't get what they want, but how when handled the right way, it doesn't have to affect you negatively. A lot of life lessons learned!

Within a few weeks, once again we packed up and headed back down to Georgia to live in a town called Jackson. It was back to words and phrases like: *hey y'all, fixin', bless your heart, yonder, ain't, cain't.* Back to biscuits & gravy and boiled peanuts. I knew the drill! I wasn't too scared. I knew the change would still be a challenge, but I was up for it...for the most part!

Thankfully, it was the summer before my junior year of high school when we got to Jackson. I was glad I didn't have to jump into starting school right away. I still absolutely hated being the new girl at school!

Our new church, Abundant Life was very excited about our family being there; everyone was so welcoming to us. We started getting all settled into our new home.

My mom was such a pro at unpacking and setting up a house that she had it down in no time! Mom usually let my sister Katie and I set up our room by ourselves, and that was fun for me. I loved being able to get creative and organize everything just like I wanted it!

I made friends at church very quickly, and it was a bit of a relief that most of them would be going to the same school that I would be starting soon. This time, my clothes were in fashion, my teeth were straightening out with braces, and I had a little more confidence after going through what I had gone through living in the other place. I was feeling pretty good and I wasn't as concerned with what people were doing or thinking as much. The adjustment of moving to Jackson wasn't as painful... at first.

It also didn't hurt that one of the deacons' sons was around my age, and I had an immediate crush on him as soon as I saw him! In my *fairy tale* mind, I was certain he was "the one." I thought, WHY on earth wouldn't he be the one? He was cute, he was a Christian, he was a drummer and a singer, and his family went to our church. Sounded perfect to me! Well, my wish came true. Bryce, the deacons' son, became my boyfriend. All of the sudden, living back in Georgia was the best decision ever!

I was almost 16, and I had never had a first kiss or a boyfriend. This was definitely not the case with other girls my age. I was really behind in the whole *boy* thing compared to some, but not to me. I always wanted my first kiss to be special. I didn't just want to make out with whomever said that I was pretty. Since I had convinced myself that Bryce was "the one"... I fell in love immediately. I fell head first, like way over the top.

I don't know girls, have you ever had a glimpse of your storybook ending with someone and then you put your heart in your hand and give it to that person because you think it's safe? Wow, that was a crazy long sentence...but it was just like that! It was crazy, but I was smitten!

A few weeks before school started, I got my first kiss and it was awesome. It wasn't awkward or lustful or at a party playing spin the bottle. It was also ok with my parents. They were actually happy for me when I told them about it! Ahhh, young love. I am glad that I waited for such a sweet moment and that I didn't start all of that boy stuff too soon. Don't grow up too soon girls! Life happens soon enough. Those moments should be memorable and precious. Don't waste them!

Summer was coming to an end, and I was looking forward to school starting in the Fall. Except... two weeks before school started, Bryce dumped me. I guess the guy I had convinced myself was "the one" was not the one at all. I was heartbroken. My mom consoled and assured me that everyone goes through heartbreak at least once in their life. I was trying to make sense of it, since I was new to the whole boy thing.

So, are you wondering *why* I was dumped? It all became clear to me once school started. Bryce wanted to get back together with his one true love and I was the wrong *Kelly*. He was actually madly in love with another girl named Kelly, who he had dated before I moved to town.

I had no idea this other Kelly even existed! (That goes back to being the new girl and being thrown into other peoples' worlds.) It's ok though, girls. I got my prince later... in college. As for the other Kelly that I was dumped for? We became good friends and she was actually in my wedding years later. So, don't let life control you too much.

Okay, back to the point. Enough talking about boys! Well, kind of... I'll probably talk about them a few more times in this book. (Wink)

I was happy to finally start my 11th grade year. I was a junior in high school and I could not believe it! Even though I was starting a new school, I didn't feel as scared as I had in the past. I had grown so much with God and He had really helped me understand the truth in this verse:

Philippians 4:13- For I can do everything through Christ who gives me strength.

A nice girl from my church met me in the morning on the first day of school. She was nice enough to introduce me to all of her friends. It was too bad though, because all of them were sophomores and I didn't have classes with any of them. The only thing I was feeling nervous about was finding my classes. The school wasn't big, but I still didn't like not knowing where I was going.

A tall boy with a nice smile named Jake, walked right up to me and introduced himself. He asked if he could walk me to my classes. I was so relieved! Not just because this boy was cute, but because someone was actually going to help me! Jake was really easy to talk to, and he seemed to be a super nice guy. I also found out that Jake was a Christian, and we ended up having a lot of things in common. Jake helped me get where I needed to go, and waited for me outside of each class. Thank God for him, because not one single girl in my homeroom even said hello to me. They just kind of looked at me, like who are you?

I decided I wasn't going to let it ruin my day... I was used to that look when starting a new school, and I didn't want to allow others to control how I felt.

Girls, you've got to stop worrying about what your peers think. It's important that you please God first and not others. Focus on yourself, who you are and who you want to become. Now, I'm not saying to become selfish and *only* focus on yourself.

Remember this... You can't change people, and you cannot control how they treat you. You have to stop worrying about the people who treat you badly or speak negatively to or about you. Give it to God! I had to learn this very early on in my life and it has saved me from so much frustration as an adult. Pray for them, and use those insecure moments to allow God to strengthen your character and *who* you are! You cannot control the way that people respond to you. So give it to the One who can.

No matter how old you are, there will always be a critic out there. As you put more effort into your relationship with God, He will help you to develop a love for yourself, and *true* confidence will begin to build.

There is a lot to be learned from always being the "new girl." There are two types of personalities that frequent new environments (especially with girls). One type of personality is one that is friendly and excited to make new friends. This personality type is not jealous or competitive with others. This personality type is intrigued by learning, and that includes learning about people and other places.

The second type of personality is one that doesn't like change and is uncomfortable with anything new, including new people. People with this type of personality may reject new people or experiences to avoid discomfort. The thought of stepping out of the comfort zone or someone being better than them makes them treat others badly or causes them to pull away to save themselves discomfort. They sometimes may be jealous, competitive and maybe judgmental.

It would be great if we could all *not* be the second personality. There is not a whole lot of personal growth that can come if we stay around the same people and the same environments our whole lives. Being outside of our comfort zones is the only way to learn new things and grow as a person. Don't be afraid! Do new things! Meet new people! Learn about them and try to understand them without judging.

So, back to the first day of 11th grade. That dreaded lunch hour was approaching. My new friend Jake didn't have my lunch hour, and I wondered who I would sit with since no girl had even said hello to me yet. I had already resigned myself to the fact that I would probably be sitting alone. Oh well, I had sat alone before... I guess I would live.

Then during Spanish class, I heard, "Psssst...Hey girl!" I looked up and this cute spunky girl was standing at my desk. She said, "Hey girl, I've been waiting to meet you. I saw your picture in the newspaper. Isn't your daddy the new pastor at that church?" (Our family picture was actually in the local paper welcoming us to the town...

I told you it was small.) Without even asking, this girl looked at me and said, "I'm Lise, and you're gonna sit with me at lunch, okay?" I was so relieved! I quickly answered "O.K.!" So, Lise and I ate lunch outside together. Lise was easy to talk to, and I loved her confidence and style.

The next day at school, I had a couple of people from the "popular" table ask me to sit with them. I told them that I was sitting outside with my new friend Lise. This "popular" kid started laughing at me and informed me that I would get a bad reputation if I sat outside, because only certain types of people sit outside for lunch. Since I was new to the school I didn't know all of the little inside "rules" and quite honestly, I didn't care. The popular kid informed me that the only people who sat outside were the black people and the Mexicans, or the ones who date them. I was thinking, Whhhaatt? I couldn't believe what I was hearing. Here we go again. Racism and prejudice. I didn't and still don't have time for it. These people had no idea of my background and my roots.

They made rude comments about me being a "yankee" and they didn't even know me. Making fun of me just made them feel more comfortable and in control. I knew that. Truth is, I didn't know them either. I didn't know what it felt like to live in the same small town my whole life and go to school with the same people since Pre-K. What I *did* know though was that out of everyone in the school, the only person who went out of their way to speak positively to me were two people. One of them was Lise, and I wasn't going to *not* sit with her at lunch because of a label someone had put on her race.

I told the popular kid: "I like Lise, we are friends, and I'm going to sit with her." End of story. This kid said, "Well, then people will think you are like her, so watch out." I responded: "Who cares?"

It's hard when you are surrounded by people who are gossiping in your ear, trying to form *your* opinions of other people. A lot of times the people who go out of their way to report bad information about someone else are usually the ones who have the issues.

This holds true with people you encounter now in your teen years, and it's true with people you will encounter in your adult years. People would tell me all kinds of crazy stories about others in that school. Since I had never lived around any of these people, I never knew what to believe. All I knew to do was to follow God, my instincts and tried to be myself as much as possible.

After all the moves I had been through, I had never lived anywhere where so many rumors were flying around about other people. A few times I was dumb enough to believe those rumors and even hurt someone in the process of believing lies. It was literally my first experience with such extreme gossip, BUT I sure did learn from it.

Life Lesson: Don't always believe what others are telling you about someone. Form your own opinions and get the facts for yourself. It goes back to what I was saying earlier...A lot of times insecure people will tell you things to make themselves feel better, or because they themselves are trying to fit a certain mold or look a certain way.

As the year went on, Lise and I became great friends. Lise started coming to church with me, and I was able to lead her to receiving the Lord into her life. She and I made many great memories together! Lise is and always will be one of my dearest friends. What a wonderful person and friend I would have missed out on knowing if I would have been more concerned about fitting into the "popular" crowd.

You see girls, you have to look to the future in the relationships that you make. Don't live for the moment or be friends with people to gain "status." It will be a waste of time, emotion and energy. There were a couple of girls I tried being friends with because they were popular, and it got me nowhere. In the end, I only felt unwanted, insecure and left out. "Mean girls" can be so competitive because they may worry that someone will *one-up* them. It can be hard for them to get past their own ego enough to truly appreciate who you are.

Don't be a mean girl! I tried being a mean girl to someone once. It's not cute and it breaks God's heart. God wants us to look past stereotypes, racism and prejudice. He wants us to love one another and treat one another kindly. When I look back, I am so thankful that I never treated anyone differently because they were a different color or background than me. That was a choice I made, and you can too.

Thankfully, we didn't move again and I was *finally* able to graduate from high school! God helped me get through those last two years of high school with a lot of grace and a whole lot of learning experiences. Finally, I could start looking at college! I was glad to be an official adult. After graduation, I left Jackson, Georgia to go to college in Springfield, Missouri where I knew absolutely no one...again. This time though, it was my choice to do so.

This new adventure and change was my decision, and not someone else's decision for me. I left the place where I had my first boyfriend, my first kiss, first fell-in-love, first got my heart broken, first got to be a cheerleader, first got my driver's license, first passport, first car, first car payment and first real date. I learned to not listen to gossip. I also experienced a taste of teenage freedom cruising up and down the little town of Jackson in my blue car!

There sure was a lot of change throughout my first eighteen years of life. I had lived in thirteen houses or apartments in six cities, all within three states. There were lots of people coming and going in and out of my life, along with new environments to explore. The only thing that was always constant was the love and friendship of Jesus. I am thankful for the growing process, changes and experiences...the good ones, and the bad ones.

There are moments in your life when you will be uncomfortable. There are moments of doubt, insecurity, hurt, unanswered questions and seemingly unanswered prayers.

These moments will most definitely always be there. It's what you choose to do in those moments and with those feelings that will develop your character. You can choose to run away, back down, wallow in self-pity and speak negatively. Or you can choose to allow God to strengthen, teach and truly mold you. "How do I do that?" you may ask.

1) **Don't be afraid.** Life is going to happen and it won't always be perfect. Try and embrace the changes life brings...no matter

how uncomfortable it feels. Allow life experiences to become like a trampoline that propels you to go higher than you could just staying in one safe place!

2) **Don't doubt yourself.** Unless the Lord is convicting you in an area, never let other people's comments or negativity bring you down. Seek what God would have you to change about yourself. Be confident that He loves you and knows everything you will ever go through.

3) **Live it out!** Don't hide the strength and confidence God has given you. Show it! Not in arrogance or obnoxiousness, but in humility and grace. Remember, you could not get through situations in life without the Lord. So doesn't He deserve all the credit? Let that light shine, regardless of how dark life may seem at times.

4) **Most importantly, *Go to God first*.** Friends are very important at your age, but they do not have all of the answers! Before

you spill your guts to your friends hoping for solutions, go to *THE* solution....Jesus! When you put Him first, you will truly start to feel like He is your best friend. It won't be a cliche' anymore: "Jesus is my Best Friend," He Will Be!! Yeah Jesus!!

Do some soul searching and think about these areas of your life for a minute.

I'm Uncomfortable When This Happens:

1.

2.

3.

4.

What I Want to Learn Through It:

1.

2.

3.

4.

Ways I Commit to Praying About it:
1.

2.

3.

My prayer for you:

Lord, you know my friend inside and out. You see her struggles and you know where she is fearful. Help her to be *BRAVE*. Help her to embrace your plan, and help her to learn great things on her journey! Whatever she is going through right now, or whatever she may go through in the future, I pray for strength and determination to become a strong and brave young lady. Help her to choose joy and always embrace her inner warrior!

In Jesus Name, Amen.

Chapter 2

Finding God in Everyday Life

Do you realize that every single day is a gift from God? From the time you put your feet on the floor; God has truly given you a gift. It's called...a NEW day! Life. Whether you feel that your life is good or bad... what you choose to do with this gift of life is up to you. Reading God's Word is the easy part. Applying it can be tougher, but it is possible to do!

Do you ever feel like your life is falling apart? Ever feel like someone else has a better life? Do you feel like your life is boring and things never go your way? These are feelings you probably experience now, and will probably experience from time to time as you grow older. Annnddd...they are just that...they are FEELINGS! Feelings are not usually our reality; our feelings are always subject to change. Even staying up too late and not getting enough sleep can take your mood on a roller coaster ride... not to mention looking at Instagram and Snapchat until your eyeballs are frozen. Your mind will start to feel cluttered with what reality really is. Constantly looking at those things on social media can leave you feeling bad because people appear to be so perfect. We know the truth though! No one *just* woke up like that.

Maybe you are on the other side of these feelings. Do you feel like you are confident in yourself? Deep down, do you think you are a little better than others? Have the Instagram filters become who you try to be or who you think you are? Do you focus on having a lot of material things (clothes, shoes, jewelry, etc.) to keep up with others? Do you have an attitude as if you are better than others because you feel "confident?" It's ok to be confident, but let's dig deep and make sure you have God-confidence and not just SELF-confidence.

It's pretty tempting at this stage of your life to allow physical appearance, talents, grades, friends, clothes and other things to determine how you feel about yourself. I mean, no one likes a bad hair day.

That's why it is so important to learn about and understand yourself now as a teen. Otherwise, you will waste years of your adult life dealing with these same feelings, missing out on meaningful relationships and struggling to find yourself. I love this scripture:

1 Timothy 4:12- Don't let anyone think less of you because you are young. Be an example to all believers in what you say, in the way you live, in your love, your faith and your purity.

You are not too young to grow deeper in understanding yourself and who God has created you to be. You are not too young to change your thought process; you are not too young to be an overcomer! Don't ever let your age be an excuse not to grow and learn. I am so passionate about getting this message across to you! The only way you can be a *Resilient* girl in life is by seriously trusting and appreciating God in every situation. Being *Resilient* means that you are able to withstand and recover from difficult situations. The only way to recover or withstand any situation is with God helping you and guiding you in your life.

Trust me, your adult life will be full of ups and downs; you will be learning so many other new things. Learn whatever you can now! I believe that by learning a different thought process now, you will be able to recognize those insecure and uncomfortable feelings as an adult. You will know what triggers them, but you will also know how to hold them captive and control them before they control you. Our minds are very powerful! The devil's most annoying way to get to us, is by getting in our minds. It makes me so mad at him!

Here's what I have discovered over the years of working with both teens and adults, and also from personal experience: Sometimes adults can act just like teens. I've been in situations or had adults treat me a certain way that sent me straight back to a feeling I had in high school, and I'm like... wait...what? I thought we were adults now! I thought those days were over. Unfortunately, those days are *not* over a lot of times.

In high school, everyone seems to be separated by groups. When I was in high school, there were all types. The *popular* group, *emo* or *goth* group, the *smart* kids, *band kids* or the *in-between* group, not popular but not quite unpopular either. The problem is that sometimes these groups tend to define you in high school. You may start to feel like that the group with whom you are identified is *actually* who you are; as a result, you may find yourself keeping *yourself* in that box.

Let's give a scenario of two girls, that both mirror real life girls today:

One is a more timid, and maybe insecure girl questioning life... questioning if she dresses good enough, looks good enough, always wants more but feels less than everyone. She doesn't really make a move until someone else does because she's so afraid of not being accepted or fitting in. She's a follower and she's a little awkward but not totally "uncool." She just has a poor self-view and maybe doesn't know where she fits in. She doesn't step outside the box because she fears she may not be good enough. Let's call her "Abbie."

Then there's the more *Confident* girl who seems to have everything together. She is pretty, happy, popular... maybe she feels she's better than others or even treats people as if she is better than them. She's good at a lot of things and gets a lot of attention from her family, as well as teachers and others. She knows people are watching her and sometimes it can go to her head. This may cause her to treat anyone badly who may be a "threat" to her position or image. She may even be a little bit of a mean girl. Let's call her "Cassie."

Here is the deal: If Abbie goes through her teenage years feeling insecure, sad, less than other people, wanting what they have and keeping herself closed off from experiencing anything new, chances are that she's not taking the time to find her own strengths. Chances are she is giving into her fears, wasting so much time worried about what others are doing. She is likely to enter adulthood with the same issues. She will continue this pattern. The negative voices that had got into her head and her feelings of "not being good enough" are still controlling her feelings. She may eventually grow out of it, but may waste time in her 20's or 30's doing so. If the feelings Abbie had in high school had not controlled her so much, then who knows what she could have accomplished? How much more would she have been ready to take on, had she'd been free! Who knows? She may have even been super-talented but hid that talent for so long that she now has to start from scratch in using her abilities!

Let's compare Abbie to Cassie. Cassie is the bubbly pretty girl and may be the one who appears to have it all together. She looks good all the time and everyone seems to put her on a pedestal. She's popular and doesn't have to try too hard to make friends; people always seem eager to be her friend.

How do they compare? Usually what happens is Cassie grows into adulthood with a big shocker. Unfortunately her confidence is very superficial, heavily based on circumstances and the people around her. Her confidence is pretty much based on affirmation;

once she's not getting that affirmation, she doesn't really know what to do with herself. Her circle of influence has been very small and everyone is not that impressed once she hits college and adulthood. She can possibly begin to lose confidence once she realizes there are other people in the world just as pretty and as talented. She could begin to be insecure but tries to overcompensate for it instead. She could also begin to become competitive with others and feel sorry for herself as an adult.

See, putting too much emphasis on that high school image will mess you up later! We all change physically and I'm sorry girls, but when you hit a certain age, your high school abilities won't benefit you that much in adulthood. Have you ever seen a 40 year old cheerleader? Yikes! Let me know if you have.

Do I sound like I am being a downer? I'm really not! Promise! Seriously, I think you should have a good time and enjoy your high school years! I just don't want you to let them define you. I hope this is making sense to you. Looks are going to fade, but it is what's in your heart that matters.

So, how can the two girls in our Abbie and Cassie scenarios be helped? It's simple, but requires strategy to put into action. The answer is ... drum roll please....

YOU ARE NOTHING WITHOUT GOD! I am nothing without GOD! WE are all nothing without Him!

Everything comes from HIM. Every talent, the way you look, your personality, your sense of style, and even your place in life...God has given uniqueness to you! He made you to be YOU! He did not make you to be anyone else. If every person in the world could truly get a hold of this truth and appreciate it, life would be a little easier! The comparison trap would be non-existent, and people would *not* feel the need to imitate or measure up to a Kardashian, a Jenner or a Hadid.

You have to tell God THANK YOU and give Him Glory in your daily life. "Glory" is sort of a Christianese word, and you may be wondering what in the world does it mean to give God glory? Well, it means you must thank Him because He has won notable achievements. He has literally won a *huge* remarkable achievement by giving you everything that you have! Whether you think you have enough or not, God has a plan for your life! If you waste time complaining, then you're losing valuable moments to grow with God. You have every tool you need to succeed through Him! Ask God for confidence and strength.

God created you in His image. God did not say: "I'm going to create one better than the other." It's so important to give God credit for everything in your life... even in the bad times. If you speak to God and ask Him to pull you through, He will pull you through!

Sometimes you've gotta give Him a minute, or two...or three. God is not a microwave or a smartphone. He does things in His time. Learning patience is a part of maturing. He does need a little help from you though. A little help...meaning your heart has to know and believe that God never leaves you! You need to believe that every single moment you go through is to teach and make you stronger! If you begin to see God in the little things, then nothing you do will be about You; it will be about HIM. Your prayer and thought process won't be: "God, how could you do this to me?" It will be "God, I don't understand, but I know you are working out a plan...I know you love me... please help me understand...I put my trust in you!"

When you can grasp this reality, your confidence will grow! It will grow because you are relying and acknowledging someone who doesn't want you to fail. Bam! Did you know that? GOD DOES NOT WANT YOU TO FAIL! So awesome!! When you are acknowledging God in your life and not worrying about anyone else's opinion but His, it is so freeing! Love it!

Throughout my middle school and high school years, my parents couldn't afford to get us a lot of extra stuff (clothes, shoes, hair salon visits, makeup, etc.) I definitely had everything that I needed, but there was not a lot of frivolous spending. At Westwood High School, one of the schools I attended in New Jersey, people seemed to put a lot of importance on material things. Sometimes, some of the girls at school would check the tags in me and my sisters' shirts to see where our clothes were from. Katie and I weren't raised to place a lot of value on name brands. When the girls would check our tags, it left us feeling a little insecure. I mean, we had what we needed and we didn't go without clothes, even if they were at times, hand-me-downs. Our parents didn't let us feel sorry for ourselves. They instead showed us to count our blessings. They taught us that material things can't make us happy or fulfilled. I know my parents would have loved to take us on a big shopping spree... it just was what it was. God always provided.

While living in Newark, New Jersey, our family had become very close with my third grade teacher, Miss Walker. When we moved away from New Jersey, Miss Walker would come to Georgia to visit us. She spent many Christmases with our family as well. Every month, Miss Walker would send us what she called a "care package." These care packages were the best things ever! She would send us the most awesome box, filled with clothes, perfume, books and accessories.

My favorite item was always the brand new outfit she would send. Miss Walker had great taste! We were always so excited when our care package came in the mail. My mom would lay our things out nicely on our beds, so that when Katie and I came home from school we would see them there. We were always taught to be thankful to Miss Walker but most importantly, to be thankful to God. My parents made us aware that it was God who had provided for Miss Walker, so that she could give to us. We were also taught that it was God who put it in Miss Walker's heart to give so generously to our family. See that girls? It all goes back to God. You've got to teach yourself to recognize that. You can be thankful to a person for doing something, but at the end of the day, we have to be grateful to God for what *He* uses others to do.

I remember how good I felt about myself when I would put on my new clothes from the care package, and wear them to school. I also remember looking at myself in the mirror and thinking "God gave me these." An awesome feeling rose up inside of me, just to think that God cared about me so much. God wanted me to have this small desire of my heart so badly that He put it on someone else's heart to make it happen.

Girls, that's where building that God-confidence happens. How easy it would have been for me to just *expect* those care packages? How easy it would have been for me to think that I was "all that" in those new outfits and brag to all of my friends? It's in those moments, you have to realize God is the core source for anything you gain in life. If I would have taken those care packages for granted and not recognized God's hand in it, I would have had a false confidence. I would have been putting all of the value into myself, thinking, Look what I have or Look how good I look. Thinking like that would have put all of the focus on me. Without God, we are nothing, so why would I want the focus on me? Instead, I would think: These clothes are a gift from God. Even though I did feel confident about the way I looked in my new clothes, it really wasn't about me, but about God!

Of course, I did have parents who drilled gratefulness and thankfulness into my head. Still, even though my parents taught me those things, at some point I had to make the choice to learn God's perspective for myself. I had to make the choice to understand the concept that every good and perfect thing comes from God alone.

At a certain age, you have to make a choice to take control of your mind, thoughts about yourself and your decisions. It's a mindset that we must have to gain true confidence. It's easy to go through life day- to-day taking things for granted. Don't do it! Open your eyes and recognize God's hand. You *will* see Him...I promise!

Another way to find God in the little things is to develop a listening ear. I believe God speaks to everyone in a very personal way. It can be really easy to ignore God's voice and not even realize He's speaking.

The Lord has always spoken to me through objects, people and quiet prayer. God gives me these moments when I'm questioning Him or praying about something. If there is something specific you are praying for, or something that is on your heart, don't ever think God is not listening. He 100% is! Ask God to put hearing aids in your ears, a monitor on your heart and a check in your attitude. Finding God in the little things is about giving Him credit for everything in your life and opening your eyes and ears to see and hear Him.

Think about it. The God...our God who created Heaven and Earth...who created mankind and formed you in your mother's womb cares about *you*. Close your eyes right now and let that sink in. Let it sink into your heart and mind. God cares about the little things. He sees your heart's desires. If you pray that God will open your eyes, you will see Him in the little things. He will begin to make Himself real to you.

List 4 things that are important and personal to you.
(Hopes, Wants, Dreams)

1.

2.

3.

4.

God sees those things and He truly does care.

Psalm 37:4- Take delight in the Lord, and He will give you your heart's desires.

This was always one of my favorite scriptures. I used to write it with a scented highlighter on my brown bag covered textbooks. It's still one of my favorites and I speak it over my daughter today. It is a promise that if my heart is completely planted and rooted in the Lord, and my delight (a high degree of satisfaction) is to please Him, then He will give me the desires of my heart. Let's talk about that for a minute.

Sometimes it's easy to look at that scripture and think that it means this. "If I'm a good person then God will give me what I want". Here is what I believe and have experienced that scripture to be. If you are taking true satisfaction (delight) in the Lord, then your main goal is to please Him. Your goal is to do everything in your life to bring Him glory, to give Him the reward.

When your main desire is to please God, then the desires inside (of) your heart will be things that reflect Christ in some way. That means if you desire something specific, your desire will also be to use whatever specific thing that is, as an opportunity to share and reflect Christ. It won't be to just say, "Look at me!" God knows our intentions and He sees our hearts. There is no faking it with Him. He has the power to open and close all doors in our lives.

In my senior year of high school, I had a young new music teacher. It was her first year of teaching and she seemed to want to be "cool" or something. Her behavior was very strange for a teacher, in my opinion. This teacher very quickly picked favorites in the class. She picked a group of girls that she hung out with on the weekends and outside of school. She even wanted this select group to call her by her first name.

Calling teachers by their first name was a big no-no back in the day. You never called an adult by their first name. This select group of students would brag in front of the class about how they hung out with the teacher, and let us all know what they had done together over the weekend. I thought it was strange. Needless to say, I was not a part of the teacher's favorite group. For whatever reason, this teacher would make rude comments to me and about me in front of the class. She seemed to want to put me down. She would tell me I couldn't sing well and single me out constantly.

I can't say that I believed anything she said about me, though it did bother me. I just couldn't understand why she was saying these things. I was very passionate about music and singing. Over the years, I would get asked to sing at the schools, churches and in communities where we had lived. Sometimes the teachers would even give time at the end of class, and let me sing to everyone. The other students would put in requests and then I would bring my boom box and cassette tape collection to class. Hey, they either wanted to hear me sing or they wanted to cut the length of class by ten minutes. Either way, I loved it! I would also get stopped at my locker and be asked to belt out a song on the spot. I would do that too! Singing was like my hobby.

Because I was getting cheered on by others to sing, and because I had ears myself... I really didn't understand why my music teacher was so negative to me. It was completely frustrating! As a teen, I expected more from an adult. Still, I continued to take the music class and sing in the concert choir at the school.

Girls, I learned the art of "Shake It Off" before Taylor Swift ever made a song about it, that's for sure. Not gonna lie though, there was a little part of me that wished I could win this teacher over. There was another part of me though, that really didn't care about her opinion. Either way, I tried to always remain respectful to my teacher. I knew God had given me the gift to sing and I was very passionate about using my gift. No one was going to take that from me.

That same year, I decided to try out for the school play. I auditioned for the lead role. Go big or go home, right? Ha! The lead role was of a beautiful maiden who would wear fancy dresses on stage and get her one true love! However, one of the music teacher's favorites was auditioning for the lead role as well. Somehow, I already knew I would not get the part. It almost made me not want to even audition for the play anymore... instead I decided to do a second audition for a different role just in case I didn't get picked for the lead. Well, my intuition was right. I was given the role of an old lady who needed to look ugly and undesirable, as well as be somewhat of a nuisance. In the actual play no one wanted this character around and she was sort of the brunt of all the jokes. Ugh...not the role I had hoped for.

At the end of the day, I decided to be glad to have gotten a part in the play at all, and just move on. I decided to put my best effort into learning my role and to do my best anyway. The teacher made me feel inadequate at rehearsals, but I pushed through. I prayed that God would help me in creating this character, and help me enjoy participating because regardless, I did love the stage!

There were moments when my heart would sink, when I would overhear the teacher praising everyone else. I never heard the words "good job" and very seldom did she ever make eye contact with me. I went through that entire play wondering if I was doing a good job, or playing the part well. All I knew was that I was enjoying myself.

During that experience I once again was completely relying on the Lord for strength and encouragement. This scripture was playing in my mind over and over:

Colossians 3:23- Work willingly at whatever you do, as though you were working for the Lord rather than for people.

I decided to do my best and being a part of the play ended up being so much fun! Even though I had a great time, I still never heard a "great job" or anything positive from my teacher after the play was over. I left feeling good about my performance, but not getting approval from my teacher when I heard her praising others, made me start to doubt myself.

Here is the best part of this story... The following school day, after the play was over, an article came out in the school paper. What I read was a direct "great job" from God Himself. It was a play review written by another teacher in the school. The article totally validated my heart, my intentions, and showed me this:

Romans 8:31- What shall we say about such wonderful things as these? If God is for us, who can ever be against us?

The article went through reviewing all performances and at the end stated: "The star of the show however, was Kelly McLucas. I was very impressed with Kelly's acting and singing..."

Girls, this is a testimony! Yes, it is. It is a personal testimony between me and God. See, no one else knew how I was feeling. No one else knew how much that article spoke to me. Only me, my mom and God knew. You see a testimony isn't just someone getting up and talking about a near death experience or how God saved them from drugs. A testimony is literally anything in your life that God does for *you*. I saw it as a testimony.

I knew I had not been given the star role that I had desired, but I delighted in the Lord throughout that entire experience. In the end, He gave me the desire of my heart! By that time though, my attitude had changed because it became about God helping me be my very best and not just about me being the "star." I remember how excited my parents were to see me in the play. I realized that God validated me in a way that the teacher would not.

Another eye-opening, God moment that happened to me when I was a teen: One Christmas I asked for a gold ring. It may seem silly to some, or like okayyy big whoop, a gold ring! Well, it was not an affordable gift for my parents to get me at the time. One day when my aunt and uncle were visiting from New Jersey, Aunt Carolyn pulled out a gold ring. She asked my mom if one of us girls would want it. The ring had been in lost and found at their church for a long time and no one had claimed it. My mother immediately said yes! She was so happy because now my Christmas wish could be fulfilled.

Christmas morning came and I got my gold ring. It was the most beautiful ring I had ever seen! My mom did not tell me the details at the time, but she let me know that God gave me that ring. She told me to always remember when I looked at it that it truly was a gift from God. My new ring was very special to me.

One day, I was at a friend's house and we were in a fishing boat on a small pond that was connected to their property. It was a mucky pond and I can't even believe we swam in that thing. Gross! Anyway, we were jumping off of the boat and into the water, when I noticed that my ring was gone. I ran into the house crying and we all went back out to the pond to try and find it. I finally gave in to the fact that I had been irresponsible and that the ring was gone. So, we stopped looking. That pond was full of lily pads and thick Georgia clay (a.k.a. really thick mud)!

Weeks passed, and from time to time I would pray that God would help me find that ring. One particular Sunday, I remember praying that very prayer. After church, I went to my friend Julie's house to hang out. While I was there, my Mom called to tell me that my ring had been found! She said that our friends who owned the pond were out fishing when their son saw something sparkle in the water. He picked it up only to find that it was the ring I had lost over a month ago! That was crazy, considering the chances of something like that just floating to the surface. That was God!

As my Mom was telling me this news, I said: "Mom, I literally just prayed again today that I would find that ring!" Coincidence? I think not! God cared. He cared about that little piece of my life and that small desire of my heart. I still wear the ring today, and it is a reminder to me that God cares and He is with me always.

Girls, you will never, ever go wrong when your sole purpose and intention is to please the Lord. He will come through every time. If you look at the big picture, you will always see the hand of God. Pray that He will help you to recognize Him. There are things that He does on a daily basis for you, but you have to recognize it. Stop looking for some majestic *God moment*, and start by recognizing the little things He does for you.

I really could go on and on with story after story about how finding God in the little things helped me keep the right perspective. Seeking Him and listening for His voice helps us to grow and develop into who He wants us to be. If you don't give God a place in your everyday life, and talk to Him about the things that matter to you, you are missing out on some special moments with your heavenly Father.

Girls, don't ever let the devil make you think that anything is too big or too small for God! The faithfulness of our Heavenly Father is so constant. Don't give up just because you've prayed for something and it hasn't happened yet. Keep praying, keep trusting and keep looking for God to show up! Once you begin to recognize that EVERY good and perfect thing comes from HIM, then you will have a sense of confidence in knowing that He has your best interest at heart. Look for His hand! Listen for His voice! He is there!

James 1:17 - Whatever is good and perfect is a gift coming down to us from God our Father, who created all the lights in the heavens. He never changes or casts a shifting shadow.

Jesus is your true BFF.

List some ways you can start incorporating God into your everyday life more:

1.

2.

3.

What are some things that hinder (stop you) from hearing God's voice or feeling Him near? (E.g. Music, TV, Phones, Social Media, Friends)

1.

2.

3.

4.

Chapter 3

Forgiving Others

Have you ever been hurt by someone? Did the pain feel and seem unbearable? As human beings with feelings, we are bound to be hurt at some point in our lives. If you've been lied to, talked about, bullied or abused by someone, then you know firsthand how awful that can feel.

Sometimes I watch TV counseling shows such as Dr. Phil. On these shows, I've seen teen girls acting like they are hard-core, unaffected by people. I've seen them display an attitude, as if they don't care about anything or anyone. Have you ever watched any shows like that? Usually, parents bring their teens onto the show to see if Dr. Phil can help them. The sad thing about most of these cases is that these girls are acting out of the hurt, pain and rejection they feel in their lives.

They may have not been able to forgive those who hurt or abused them. They may not be able to process the things that happen to them in a healthy way so they in turn act like no one can hurt them. All the while, they are crying on the inside. I often want to bust through the TV and help these girls. They just want to feel loved, heard and understood. Maybe you can relate to these girls...

Did you know that forgiving others can actually add years to your life? Living with unforgiveness is a source of stress. Stress is bad...real bad. Stress causes anxiety which can trigger fear and depression. Stress can make you feel a little crazy. Those who are in a stress cycle of making bad choices, may choose to turn to drugs and other addictive substances. It may be tempting for them to want to numb the pain of an unfortunate event that took place in their lives. They may have never gotten over it, and maybe they never forgave someone who hurt them. They may even shove the feelings down inside, thinking they will go away with time...but they don't.

I've also noticed that those who live in insecurity or who are very critical and negative, have usually never gotten over a hurtful time in their life. Maybe they were even treated badly by their parents growing up... so they repeat a pattern.
If you can relate to this, I wish I could talk with you face to face, and tell you I'm sorry and that it's not your fault. Unfortunately, people will fail you and sometimes hurt you. Let me just keep it real with you girls right now...

If the world was perfect, and everyone in it was perfect,
we would have picture perfect
lives; everything would be lollipops
and rainbows.
That is not reality.
But it's OK.
It's going to be OK.

The Bible tells us that in this world we would have trouble, but Jesus Christ has overcome.

John 16:33- I have told you all this so that you may have peace in Me. Here on earth you will have many trials and sorrows. But take heart, because I have overcome the world.

You see, the Lord wants to use unfortunate experiences in your life to make you stronger and wiser. It is not His desire for you to stay stuck in a rut or to use a past experience as an excuse to sin. Our struggles are not excuses for us to whine and complain. It's understandable to go through a time of grieving, hurting, questioning and processing. However, it's not healthy to bottle up emotions and *not* deal with them. I encourage you to pray to God and talk with someone you can trust!

Journaling is also a good way to process things. Sometimes it's easier to write out your feelings than it is to speak about them. Part of the forgiving process is releasing. However, you can't release if you keep bottling up the feelings inside of your heart. It's really tempting just to run to your best friend and pour your heart out. Friends can be there for you, but if you have gone or are going through something serious, please talk to a mature adult who can help you. Don't just talk to your friends because they usually don't have real ways of helping you.

Friends are great, but friends your age are probably trying to figure life out just like you are. Sometimes they can hurt the situation more than help it. A parent, pastor or pastor's wife, teacher, school counselor or older family member are all great examples of people that you can talk to.

Forgiveness is a choice. It's not a feeling that comes over you...It's not always something you will be asked for. Forgiveness is not always something you will want to do. A lot of people don't know even know how to apologize. Apologizing takes humility and responsibility. "I'm sorry you took it that way..." or "I'm sorry you felt that way..." is not a true apology. A true apology says, "I'm sorry I hurt your feelings. I shouldn't have made you feel that way. I am sorry." Taking responsibility is key. Otherwise you're basically just saying the other person has the problem.

Maybe someone owes you an apology and you've never received it. If they would just say a simple "I'm sorry," then you could move on. Well, unfortunately that may not happen. Sometimes, people are too prideful to admit when they are wrong. They might even be unaware that they hurt you; or it could be that they just don't care. That is tough.

In a perfect world, we would all get along. Unfortunately, the world won't be that way until we are in heaven. Maybe you need to apologize to someone. A parent, friend, family member, teacher, pastor or church leader? Maybe you even need to forgive *yourself* for something.

Here is a story about a time I had to ask for forgiveness. In my senior year of high school, I had this boyfriend. His name was Kyle. I was crazy in love with Kyle, and I was sure we would be married one day. Since I was so crazy in love with this boy, I was also crazy and jealous every time he talked to this certain girl named Sarah. It used to make me so mad! Maybe it made me mad because she was clearly flirting with my then-boyfriend. Or maybe I was worried Kyle would dump me for her? Maybe something about her in general just annoyed me; I don't know, I think it was all of those things. Even so, those were not reasons for me to treat her rudely, and I was *really* mean to Sarah.

We were never friends, but she and Kyle had a lot of the same classes together; that just made my blood boil. Anyway, I made it known that I did not like Sarah and even went over to her lunch table one day to give her a piece of my mind. Acting out that way was totally out of character for me, and I would always feel bad after I acted that way. Over the summer, Kyle and I broke up. I knew God had other plans for me, and ultimately Kyle knew it too.

I headed off to my first semester at college and while I was there, God showed me that I needed to apologize to Sarah for how I had treated her. When I came home on Christmas break, I went to visit my high school. I found out what lunch period Sarah had since another underclassmen had lunch with her. Anyway, I got a visitor pass from the office, and started walking straight towards Sarah's table. I'm sure she was shocked to see me since I had already graduated. I think I saw a little worry in her eyes, as she was trying to figure out why I was there in the first place. I walked over and said, "Hey Sarah... I just wanted to say that I am really sorry for how I treated you. That is not who I am, and I apologize." She quietly said, "Ok...thanks."

We had about three seconds of small talk and then that was that. That was the last time I ever spoke to her. Sometimes when I think back to those days, I start to feel bad for the way I acted towards her. Then I remember the part where I went out of my way to apologize, and I feel better. Hopefully, that apology also helped her feel better as well. I not only had to ask for forgiveness, but I had to forgive myself as well.

Here is the deal. Forgiveness was given to us through Jesus Christ. He literally DIED on the cross. Sometimes I imagine how scary that day must have been. I struggle even watching crucifixion re-enactments because they sort of freak me out. Jesus died for people who treated him so badly, spit on him, made fun of him, beat him, stabbed him and killed him. They were the epitome of what society calls BULLYING. *He* was bullied. Yet Jesus lovingly and obediently forgave them. Jesus was obeying His Father. His Father sent Him to go through this agony, and Jesus obeyed.

That is truly amazing love! So how come we find it so hard to forgive? I've had to choose to forgive others at a young age. I'll never understand why Christians a.k.a. Christ followers (meaning to be like Christ) hurt one another. You would think we would treat one another with the fruits of the Spirit, right? The fruits of the Spirit are love, joy, kindness, self-control and gentleness.

We should treat one another using these spiritual characteristics, but we are human. We mess up and others mess up. Even people you look up to and trust might mess up. Is there someone who has let you down or hurt you? Have you ever told them how you feel? If not, I encourage you to pray about doing so. Pray and ask God if you should speak up. Just don't go into it expecting anything. They may not apologize. They may say that you are being ridiculous, or that it never happened.

Whatever the case, I want to encourage you to move on from these hurts. Start a pattern of forgiving others in your life. You can waste a lot of time worrying and waiting for a moment to happen or words to be spoken that may never come. Determine in your own heart to forgive. Allowing your energy to be wasted on what others have done, or *are* doing to you is a huge waste of time. The

people who hurt you are in a sense controlling you, and will continue to control
you...until you forgive them in your heart.
Pray that God will help you and show you
how to move forward.

Forgive others even if they don't ask. Say:
"Lord, this person or people hurt me deeply.
I forgive them because You forgave me.
Please have Your way in my life and in the
lives of those who have hurt me." Try praying something like this every time the
thought of what was done to hurt you tries
to creep back in your mind.

Growing up in different environments, I
have experience with different groups of
people that seem to have various opinions
about me. When girls would be nasty to me
or roll their eyes at what I was wearing, I
would do something crazy... I would smile
at them! Those smiles did not always come
easily. Sometimes when I was trying to work
up the courage to smile, there were some
uncomfortable gas knots in my stomach; I

would be praying to sweet Jesus that my nerves wouldn't get the best of me...if you know what I mean.

Why smile? In those situations, I figured I had two options. One, roll my eyes back and be just as rude as them. Or two, give them what they didn't expect... a smile. In those moments, this scripture would play in my head:

Proverbs 15:1- A gentle answer turns away wrath, but a harsh word stirs up anger.

Did the smile always work? Nope. I remember this one girl who sat across from me in class. She would stare at me and mouth the words "I hate you" every time I looked up. Funny, I had only been at that school for about two weeks. How could she of "hated" me? Simple. The girl she had been friends with since kindergarten wanted to be my friend. So, she hated me.

Every time she would mouth the words "I hate you," I would give her a big smile. The smile didn't mean that I didn't care, because it hurt my feelings that she was saying these things. The smile meant, I won't let you get to me. The smile meant, You can be mean all day girlfriend, but I'm going to choose to be nice. For six months, I dreaded going to school. Eventually the girl that "hated" me started wanting to be my friend.

In life, you have to make tough choices. Who do you choose to be? How do you choose to treat others? Jesus had every right to beat His bullies until they were black and blue. Oh, and He sure could have. But He didn't. He chose to love. We have to choose to love too... just like Jesus. Ask God to help you get to the root of your unforgiveness, insecurity and fear. Be honest with Him. You must forgive because God has a great purpose for you to walk in! You don't want that junk holding you back!

Who do you need to forgive? Write their names down and write in what way they hurt you. Get that stuff out, girlfriend!

People I need to forgive...

I'm hurt because they...

I believe God wants me to forgive because...

Ways I can Activate Forgiveness...

Chapter 4

Loving Yourself

While living in New Jersey during my sophomore year of high school, I had a crush on a boy at my church. His name was Drew. Drew loved God and didn't make that a secret. Drew outwardly expressed his love for God in worship and in the way he treated others. I would wonder if he liked me too... I mean I wasn't allowed to date yet, but when you have a crush you do tend to wonder if your crush likes you too.

One of Drew's friends named Aaron was in my study hall class at school. Aaron was a little rude and seemed arrogant. He thought he was God's gift to all girls. Do you know any boys like that? Every day during study hall, Aaron just didn't seem to be happy *unless* he was teasing me. He would say things to me like: "Drew will never like you, because you're ugly." Or, "Drew will never like you because you have crooked teeth and a flat butt." Or even: "You need to get over it because Drew would never like you...he can do so much better than you."

I seriously wanted to slap this kid Aaron, but I didn't. So many times I wanted to cry, and a few times I did... However, it was that little situation in study hall as a 14 year old girl that caused to me to ask myself some important questions. I stood in front of the bathroom mirror with tears in my eyes and asked myself, "Am I pretty?" Am I good enough?" Yes, my butt was indeed flat. But did that make me ugly? No. Yes, my teeth were crooked, but did that make me ugly? No, it didn't.

I decided not to beat myself up about the way God had created me. I didn't allow some mean kid's words and opinion to become my opinion or identity. I didn't think I was ugly. What is ugly, anyway? Who defines what ugly is?

"Ugly" (on the outside) is only someone's opinion. Girls, we are all like art pieces. Every one of us is unique. Some may consider one art piece beautiful and another not so pretty. Some think modern art is beautiful, others think graffiti is beautiful, some think oil paintings with intricate details are beautiful. Beauty is really an opinion. If someone tells you you're ugly...does that mean you are? Absolutely not! Sometimes people need to keep their opinions to themselves. There is no fact sheet that states what makes a person beautiful. God's Word is the guideline that speaks of what true beauty and worth is... and by God's standards, beauty is all on the inside anyway! If others cut you down (as this boy in my study hall did to me,) those are only opinions that they should keep to themselves.

When you allow someone else's opinion to become how you feel, it can be very destructive. If someone says you're ugly and then you think you're ugly, that is *not* ok. If someone says you're stupid and then you think you're stupid... that's not okay. The flip side of that is if someone says you're pretty and then you think you're pretty... or if someone says you're smart, then you think you're smart... get where I'm going? While encouragement is beneficial and it is needed in our lives, you cannot base how you feel about yourself on everyone else's opinions.

I want to encourage you to take a good look at yourself. Be honest with yourself. If there are areas you would like to change then only you (with God's help) have the power to do so. Remember, beauty is truly on the inside. Whatever is on the outside is subject to opinion. It's also subject to change.

I remember reading an article about a model who had acid thrown on her face, causing her face to literally be burnt off. It left hideous scars all over her face as a result. What a nightmare! Can you imagine? All of a sudden what this model and those around her had placed so much worth on, was gone forever. How awful!

Girls, do you know what you have to do? It's really easy... JUST BE YOU! Be the best you possible. The truth is, if someone is putting you down or discrediting your abilities, they aren't displaying the qualities of someone whose opinion you should give credit to anyway. When I would be treated badly by others growing up, I would ask myself, Wow, this person is saying these hurtful things about me, but why? Have I hurt them? Have I judged them in words or actions? Have I been rude to them?

When I could answer *no* to these questions, I would then say that this is a *them* problem. Unless I have wronged them, there is no apparent reason for them to hurt me or be rude to me. Maybe our personalities just don't click, or maybe they have been hurt in the past and are putting up a wall with me.

The devil wants you to feel rejected...but a lot of times when others reject you, it's not really about you. We have to understand that people form opinions based on what they have been taught. They also form opinions based out of their own hurt and desire to fit in. Even though we often form opinions about others, it's still no reason to treat someone badly. Girls, pray for the "them" you encounter in life, but please don't let "them" define you.

When they put you down, smile, wave then go home and cry to God in your pillow if you have to... Pray for His love to overwhelm you. Don't retaliate and don't let "them" win by causing you to feel depressed or unloved.

I don't think I have ever met an outwardly ugly person. Seriously. Beauty is in everyone. It breaks my heart when I hear of teens taking their own lives because someone has treated them badly and hurt them.

Please, if you are cutting, or thinking about hurting yourself because of someone else's opinion of you, don't do it! *They* aren't worth it! YOU are worth it!

God made you in His image. Anyone who says you are not beautiful is unaware of who God truly is.

Remember these things:

Love yourself.

Treat yourself kindly.

Be real with yourself.

Don't lie to yourself.

Strive to better yourself.

Take steps through God's Word.

Be the best version of yourself possible!

Be your unique and awesome self!

Be someone other people look up to.

Be an encourager of those around you.

If someone puts you down, don't get mad or even.

Give them a compliment or smile and walk away.

Don't be a victim of what others say or do.

Know that you are created for a purpose.

Your dreams are not too big or too small.

God made you in His image.

Anyone who says you are not beautiful is

unaware

Of who God truly is.

This may sound crazy but sometimes you have to get over yourself, in order to love yourself. Self-loathing is an extreme dislike or hatred of yourself, or being angry with yourself. Maybe you are struggling with an eating disorder, wanting so bad to be thinner. Maybe you are cutting, or you even want to die to take away the pain in your life. Maybe you're wasting a lot of time and money on magazines or on an excess amount of make-up to feel better about yourself. These are patterns that are very harmful to you. Especially if you are physically hurting yourself... Don't battle alone!

You must not waste any more time hating yourself over things others have said or done to cause you pain. Don't waste time thinking about the bad things in your life. Don't waste time focusing on material and surface things to fill a void in your heart.

In the moments when you don't feel good enough, try listening to some worship or positive music, read the Bible or a devotional or try praying or writing a prayer in a journal. If you're being cyberbullied or Instagram and Snapchat are making you feel negatively about your life... stay off of the internet or block people until things settle down. You have to make wise choices to look out for yourself and your own mental well-being.

If something is a negative voice in your life... choose to shut it down. Girls, only you can do this for yourself. Guard your hearts and minds!

Take a minute and write down ways that you are going to start loving yourself. What are some good *loving yourself* habits that you could start in your life?

1.

2.

3.

4.

On a Side Note:

The fact that you are reading this book and haven't put it down yet shows me that you want to grow. (Wink) Thank you for being you.

Just like a caterpillar needs time to turn into a butterfly, give yourself time to grow. Don't expect everything to happen overnight. With time, prayer, and learning to smile, it will happen! God loves you sooo much. You're gonna get through it, girl!

You are BEAUTIFUL!
Love,
Kelly

Chapter 5
What's Your Story?

So, what's your story? You've read some of my story, but what's yours? Every single thing you go through is a teaching and learning moment in your life. If you flunk one of life's *tests*, instead of getting so mad that you give up or become angry with yourself, just try harder next time. Ask yourself what can I do differently? Try not to let it happen again. If it does, you keep trying! Whatever life throws your way, learn and grow.

I have certainly had my share of disappointment, pain and regret. However, I am determined to always move forward. God will bring you through anything and everything. A lot of times if things don't go our way, we want to give up. It is so much easier to quit.

It's easier to give up, cry and get attention. It takes guts and determination to rise above everything life throws at you. Allow God to change you; find Him in every single circumstance and situation.

Allow yourself to forgive and love yourself. Allow yourself to look forward, never looking back at what could have been. When I look back on things in my life, I try hard not to think: "Why did that happen to me?" I have committed over the years to trust God.

When I look back, I always reflect on what I learned and not about what happened. What did I learn? How did I grow from that experience? How have I changed because of it? Then I give God credit for what He has done in my life.

Romans 8:28- And we know that God causes everything to work together for the good of those who love God and are called according to His purpose for them.

Girls, this verse is so true. In my life when things didn't work out as I had hoped or dreamed, I still trusted God had a plan. He always did and He always does. It is so important to start this thought process now so that you can continue to grow as you become older. Don't wait until adulthood to allow God to mature your mind and thought process. Notice I keep saying "Allow?" *Allow* means to let happen or to permit. You can fight the process all day long, but allowing or giving God permission to work all things out is where the answer lies. That's where your story will begin to unfold into one of adventure and overcoming, of bravery and resilience. These qualities are truly beautiful.

Be *Brave*! Whatever the future holds, regardless of the adventure, make it count. Don't be afraid of change! Learn and change, change and learn. Move forward. Don't let your story be a repeat of those around you. Just because someone in your family struggles with certain negative behaviors or addiction does not mean you have to. Don't use the excuse: "Well, my mother or father was this way, so I am just like them". Girl, you are not them. Sure, you have their DNA, but you are your *own* person. You have the power to choose and decide how you are going to act, what you will do, and who you will be.

Be *Resilient*! Don't be a victim of other peoples' opinions or behavior towards you. Bounce back! If someone is expecting the worst from you, prove them wrong! Show them what you've got! You are a fighter and you are awesome with God's help! He is showing you His hand daily. Look for Him. Seek Him. See Him! Don't let the devil win by using people to defeat you. You have purpose, girlfriend and you have a destiny!

Be *Beautiful*! Duhhhh, because you ARE! You gorgeous girl, you! Every single hair on your head is numbered by God and He loves you so much. TV, social media and magazines are not what define true beauty. Those are only opinions. Opinions are not reality unless there are backed by facts. God's Word defines beauty, period. Those ideals that are in your face are just what someone thinks.

Be *you*! Be the best version of yourself.

Again I ask, what's your story going to be? What path do you choose? Who will you strive to become?

I am praying for you as you move forward! Believe that! I'm praying that God gives you strength and clarity. I'm praying that wounds are healed in your heart. I'm praying that love for yourself will overwhelm your heart and mind. I'm praying that you will hold God's hand so tightly and never let go. I pray that your story is a beautiful one.

Because you are her...
Brave. Resilient.Beautiful.